Praise for *Talking with God in Old Age*

Missy Buchanan is a skillful writer with the gifts of compassion and love for older persons. *Talking with God in Old Age* clearly exhibits her empathy. While the book gives voice to various storytellers, Missy's insights readily apply to anyone who is coping with aging and later life issues. Her wisdom and clarity are a gift for us all.

—**Richard H. Gentzler Jr.**, DMin
Director, Center on Aging and Older Adult
Ministries, General Board of Discipleship,
The United Methodist Church

In *Talking with God in Old Age*, Missy Buchanan captures the very essence of the journey of frailty. Her honest and inspiring meditations reflect the pain and frustration people often experience as they age into frailty. Yet within each reflection is the glimmer of hope and an acknowledgment of profound courage and strength that remains in each person regardless of his or her abilities or disabilities. The clear messages of faith, love, and grace through God's abiding presence shine

D0684828

through like a beacon of hope and understanding, and the words of the Psalms offer comfort and compassion.

—**Karla Woodward**
Pastor, Silver Link Ministries
Director, Center for Ministry with the Frail
The United Methodist Church of the Resurrection
Leawood, Kansas

There are many books about the tough problems of aging, but precious few about the spiritual gifts of aging. Missy Buchanan is a rare voice of insight and inspiration in this natural and yet anxiety-producing phase of life. *In Talking with God in Old Age*, Missy connects our need for faithful, fresh reflections on growing older with the timeless wisdom of Psalms.

—**David Crumm**
Editor, Read the Spirit (www.readthespirit.com)

Talking
with God in
Old Age
Meditations and Psalms

MISSY BUCHANAN

UPPER
ROOM BOOKS®
NASHVILLE

TALKING WITH GOD IN OLD AGE: Meditations and Psalms
Copyright © 2010 by Missy Buchanan
All rights reserved.

No part of this book may be reproduced in any manner whatsoever without written permission of the publisher except in brief quotations embodied in critical articles or reviews. For information, write Upper Room Books, 1908 Grand Avenue, Nashville, TN 37212.

The Upper Room Web site: www.upperroom.org

UPPER ROOM®, UPPER ROOM BOOKS®, and design logos are trademarks owned by The Upper Room®, a ministry of GBOD®, Nashville, Tennessee. All rights reserved.

All scripture quotations, unless otherwise indicated, are taken from the HOLY BIBLE, NEW INTERNATIONAL VERSION.® NIV®. Copyright © 1973, 1978, 1984 by International Bible Society. Used by permission of Zondervan. All rights reserved.

Scripture quotations marked NLT are taken from the *Holy Bible, New Living Translation*, copyright © 1996. Used by permission of Tyndale House Publishers, Inc., Wheaton, Illinois 60189. All rights reserved.

Scripture quotations marked NRSV are from the New Revised Standard Version Bible, copyright 1989, Division of Christian Education of the National Council of the Churches of Christ in the United States of America. Used by permission. All rights reserved.

Cover image: Thinkstock / Getty Images
Cover design: TMW Designs
Interior design: Buckinghorse Design / www.buckinghorsedesign.com
Third printing: 2011

Library of Congress Cataloging-in-Publication Data
Buchanan, Missy.
  Talking with God in old age : meditations and Psalms / Missy Buchanan.
        p. cm.
  ISBN 978-0-8358-1016-6
1. Older people—Prayers and devotions. I. Title.
  BV4580.B795 2009
  242'.65—dc22

                                                                      2009034014

Printed in the United States of America

I joyously dedicate this book to

Quintin Joseph Buchanan,

my first grandchild, born in October 2008.

Quintin, I pray you find in me

the qualities of my parents,

Mack and Minelle McGlothlin,

whose unconditional love

for their grandchildren made them

gracious, fun-filled, and faithful role models.

Contents

Acknowledgments

I would like to acknowledge the older adults at Montclair Estates Senior Residence who personally shared their lives with me during the past few years. Their transparency and faithfulness inspired me day after day. For some, the earthly journey has ended. Others continue to move forward with courage and grace. I hope that *Talking with God in Old Age* captures the authenticity of their stories, both the challenges and the joys of growing old. These older adults are my heroes!

Cornflakes

Not so long ago, this old life was
    pretty good.

A bowl of cornflakes on a familiar table.

A comfortable routine.

Then came the words that turned my
    ordinary life into a wilderness.

An unwanted diagnosis. A health crisis. A hasty
    series of appointments.

At my age, who wants one more doctor, one
    more test, one more form to fill out?

I'm worn out by worry and waiting.

I yearn to do simple tasks like making
    coffee or opening the mail.

But in this timeworn wasteland, my energy is
    spent with just a few steps.

I need a grade-A miracle.

A slam-dunk kind of miracle.

O God, rescue me from bad news.

Though I cannot see you, I trust that I am
not alone.

You are here.

Let me feel the simple wonder of cornflake
mornings once again.

Psalm 112:7 (NLT)

[Godly people] do not fear bad news;
they confidently trust the LORD to care
for them.

Frugal

When you don't know how long you'll live, it's
hard not to care about money.

Will I have enough to last me?

That question never strays far from my mind.

Some people think I'm just a cheapskate.

They snicker at my fuddy-duddy ways, like
saving coupons and taking advantage of
early-bird specials.

They don't understand why I cringe at the prices
of things.

Just thinking about money eats away at my
peace of mind.

Sure, I'd like to be more generous.

I'd like to take the family out to dinner more
often and buy the grandkids extravagant gifts.

But how do I know what I can afford?

The last thing I want to do is run out of money and become a burden to others.

If only I knew how much longer I will live!

That's the unknown in the math equation of life.

Maybe I'll live five more years. Maybe fifteen. Or maybe I'll die tomorrow.

Dear God, help me to be wise but not obsessed with thriftiness.

Help me to loosen my grip on money and to grab hold of you instead.

In the uncertainties of life, I will trust you.

For the length of my days is a sacred mystery.

Psalm 39:4-5 (NLT)

Lord, remind me how brief
my time on earth will be.
Remind me that my days are numbered—
how fleeting my life is.

You have made my life no longer
than the width of my hand.
My entire lifetime is just a moment to you;
at best, each of us is but a breath.

Rehab

I don't like rehab very much.

I don't know anyone who does.

It's hard work, especially for an old one like me.

Relearning things I already knew how to do—
    like how to walk, how to grip a ball,
    how to button my clothes.

Maybe if I were younger, I'd feel different,
    knowing I might have many years left on
    this earth.

But at my ripe age, it seems that I'm back at
    square one.

The hall is lined with folks just like me,
    most of us waiting to halfheartedly take
    our turn.

Some say rehab is for my own good.

So easy for them to say! So frustrating for me.

I wish I could close my eyes and be healed.

I am out of steam and out of courage.

It's almost more than I can bear.

Then you remind me, Lord, that we were not
   intended to carry our burdens alone.

Lift up my head so I can see the face of the
   therapist who goes beyond kindness.

Lift up my head to see the resident who gives an
   encouraging thumbs-up.

Stir my determination. Give me strength for
   another day's journey.

Then give me grace enough to share with others
   along the way.

Psalm 121:1-2

I lift up my eyes to the hills—
where does my help come from?
My help comes from the Lord,
the Maker of heaven and earth.

Once upon a Time

The pictures on the glossy brochure show
   older adults playing tennis and dancing in
   sparkly clothes.

They seem to be having the time of their lives.

That was me too, once upon a time.

But not now.

I admit, it was a delicious sliver of time.

Back then, I went on bus tours to see the
   fall foliage.

I shopped for the grandkids till I dropped.

Life was all about another outing,
   another round of golf.

But somewhere between then and now,
   things changed.

My limbs became stiff, my mind less alert.

Now I've come to accept the fleeting stages of
   old age.

Talking with God in Old Age

There is no use in skirting the truth:
    If you live long enough, aching bones and
    slow steps will come.

So on this long journey, O God,
    let my heart be youthful
    though my body is not.

Give me a thriving spirit until the very end.

Psalm 92:12-15

The righteous will flourish like a palm tree,
    they will grow like a cedar of Lebanon;
        planted in the house of the Lord,
    they will flourish in the courts of our God.
        They will still bear fruit in old age,
            they will stay fresh and green,
        proclaiming, "The Lord is upright;
            he is my Rock,
        and there is no wickedness in him."

Toss and Turn

Sometimes I dread going to sleep because I'm
   afraid I'll wake up too soon.

I don't want to look at the clock, but I can't
   help myself.

It will probably say two- or three-something.

Then I will have an argument with myself:

Go to sleep. I can't.

Close your eyes. They *are* closed, but I still
   can't sleep.

Try harder. I am!

In the dark silence, my imagination churns wildly.

Every little worry gets magnified into
   an impossibility.

My mind turns over thought after thought,
   like a tiller turning over winter dirt for a
   spring garden.

Talking with God in Old Age

Regret. Guilt. Fear. Loneliness. What if . . . ?

I am tired, and still the night drags on.

Then I realize it all comes down to this:

Can I trust you, God? Can I trust you to be who
you say you are?

Let me relax in the assurance that you are bigger
than my greatest worry.

With you I am safe.

Bring peaceful sleep to this weary old body.

Psalm 4:8

I will lie down and sleep in peace,
for you alone, O Lord,
make me dwell in safety.

Swimming in the Dark

I feel like I'm swimming in the dark.

On a moonless night, my frail arms and legs thrash about in black despair.

I can't see where I'm going or where I've been.

I can't see the danger lurking beneath the surface, but I know it's there.

I am terrified of losing what little independence I have left.

I grope for a glimmer of purpose to keep me afloat, but I cannot find it.

Floundering. Gasping for air.

In thick water I can feel but cannot see.

Then I sense your voice speaking to me, stirring my soul:

"Look up, child.

Put your feet on the rock bottom.

It is solid ground. Holy ground.

Stand up and live."

Psalm 40:2

[God] lifted me out of the slimy pit,
out of the mud and mire;
he set my feet on a rock
and gave me a firm place to stand.

My Plot of Sky

No one can take away the plot of sky I can see
from my window.

It is your gift to me, God.

Each morning I unwrap it anew.

I delight in the mellow hues that come with
breaking dawn.

Often my plot of sky is a striking blue with only
a thin puff of cloud in sight.

I like it too when an occasional fog hangs like a
misty shroud.

And on hot afternoons, the view is dark and
mysterious as menacing storm clouds rumble
in the distance.

In my little space, I watch for stars to pierce the
night sky.

An ever-changing piece of art, framed by the
window in the room where I spend my time.

There I see your glory unfurled, never to be
   repeated in exactly the same way.

There I meet you day after day.

You, the remarkable artist of my little patch
   of sky.

Psalm 19:1

The heavens declare the glory of God;
the skies proclaim the work of his hands.

Do-over

Is it too late for a do-over?

Another chance to give life a fresh start?

I've come to the end of my frail self, and
   I wonder,

Am I a spiritual failure?

When you get old, it seems all you have
   is time.

Time to think.

Time to wonder about how well you've lived
   your life.

Time to worry about people you've hurt and
   decisions you've made.

I am so weary of my weakness.

How many times will I beat my head against
   the same wall?

If I had it all to do over again, I would
   live differently.

Talking with God in Old Age

But what can I do about it now that my life is
   drawing to a close?

I need to know if you can really handle the truth
   of my life, Lord.

I confess my foul-ups and my failures and want
   to make them right.

Restore me, God of second chances.

Psalm 25:7

Remember not the sins of my youth
and my rebellious ways;
according to your love remember me,
for you are good, O Lord.

My Little Room

It is where I live now.

An institutional room in a senior care facility.

A place where every room is dreadfully alike
 except for the number on the door.

A twin bed and nightstand. A chest of drawers.

A window and an easy chair.

It's a nice-enough place with good-enough food.

But it doesn't feel like home. Not really.

Not even with the photos of my family hanging
 on the wall.

Sometimes it seems that I've become a
 silent waste,

that I've outlived my usefulness.

Down the hall are people I have heard but
 never met.

I suppose they're just sitting in their rooms too.

O God, is it true that you have a special place in your heart for old folks like us?

Come to this room where I grapple with this hard season of life.

Come grapple with me.

Psalm 142:3

When my spirit grows faint within me,
it is you who know my way.

In the Mirror

Old age crept up so slowly, I hardly noticed.

One day I was middle-aged. Then I was old.

Now I look at the image in the mirror and
wonder how I got this way.

I barely recognize myself.

Sagging head and stooped shoulders.

Gray-haired and frail.

This tent of a body has served me well, but now
it is tattered and worn.

I think you must see me better than I see myself,
Lord.

Can you still use an old body like mine?

To smile through a wrinkled face?

To caress a child with my liver-spotted hands?

Give me fresh motivation for today.

And purpose until I'm all used up.

Psalm 71:18

Even when I am old and gray,
do not forsake me, O God,
till I declare your power to the next generation,
your might to all who are to come.

Pain

Every day I wake up to pain.

Even before I open my eyes, I hunker down,
    ready to do battle.

By midmorning the agony creeps through my
    body until it reaches my soul.

Medication helps, but eventually it grinds
    me down.

Now and then it seems the pain will never end.

In this anguish, I wonder if you have forgotten me.

How long will it go on?

This is no way to live. No way to die.

You have seen the grimace on my face, God.

You have heard my moans.

Come near. Comfort me.

Don't let this searing pain rob me of joy.

Have mercy on these brittle old bones.

Talking with God in Old Age

Psalm 6:2-4

Be merciful to me, LORD, for I am faint;
O LORD, heal me, for my bones are in agony.
My soul is in anguish.
How long, O LORD, how long?

Turn, O LORD, and deliver me;
save me because of your unfailing love.

Naps

Most days, I'm ready for a nap as soon as I finish breakfast.

Just getting dressed wears me out.

I think naps are a pleasure earned from living a long life.

They're a way to escape for a while without guilt—time doesn't exist until you open your eyes again.

On difficult days, I am anxious to finish the last bite of lunch so I can get to my favorite easy chair.

I can hardly wait to sink down into the well-worn cushions and prop up my leaden legs.

My chair is my haven—a safe place where I can rest this heap of weary bones.

I secretly hope that no one will see me with my mouth gaped open.

There in my easy chair, I close my eyes to the troubles of the world, at least for a while.

Thank you for the gift of naps and the relief they bring.

Psalm 62:5

Find rest, O my soul, in God alone;
my hope comes from him.

Grumpy Moments

I am madder than a hornet!

My tablemate got served long before I did, and
the oatmeal cookies have raisins.

I confess that I'm upset and grumpy.

Sometimes when old age has gotten me down, I
complain to anyone who will listen and even
to some who won't.

But as soon as the words come out, I wish I could
reel them back in.

Why do I work myself into a dither over such
unimportant things?

In my crankiness, have I missed the blessings of
growing old?

Forgive this woe-is-me attitude, dear God.

When I am miffed, help me dust off my
better self.

Show me something to chuckle about.

Give me patience for caregivers and family
members who have problems of their own.

And remind me that I can eat around the raisins.

Psalm 86:5-7

You are forgiving and good, O Lord,
abounding in love to all who call to you.
Hear my prayer, O Lord;
listen to my cry for mercy.
In the day of my trouble I will call to you,
for you will answer me.

I Haven't Always Been Old

I haven't always been old.

I suppose it just seems that way to people at the
    senior center where I live.

Not so long ago, I had thick, chestnut-brown hair.

My knees were limber, and I could jog with ease.

But here at the center, people have only known
    me as the gray-hair in room 205.

It's as though I came to this place without a past.

What about all the things I did in my younger days?

Don't they matter?

Things like hula dancing and fly-fishing.

Or that I owned my own business and married
    my high school sweetheart.

Around here, it seems your identity doesn't begin
    until you're eighty.

But God, you know every inch of the terrain of
    my long life.

It's a story that began decades ago.

I am not just another gray-hair. I am more than a room number.

I have stories to share about how you've been faithful in life's ups and downs.

Others have stories too.

Give me a renewed appreciation for long life.

Because what I do each day really does matter to you.

Psalm 71:6-9

From birth I have relied on you;
you brought me forth from my mother's womb.
I will ever praise you.
I have become like a portent to many,
but you are my strong refuge.
My mouth is filled with your praise,
declaring your splendor all day long.
Do not cast me away when I am old;
do not forsake me when my strength is gone.

With One Eye Open

O Lord, for years, I've tried to wrap my mind
    around the big questions of faith—

questions about why you allow suffering
    and why you didn't stop a certain tragedy
    from happening.

Now I have another question to add to the list.

Why have you left me on this earth for so long?

I feel utterly useless.

And so I pray with one eye open, always mindful
    of doubts that crowd my thinking.

One eye open, as though I'm keeping tabs
    on you.

As if you owe me an explanation.

As if I can't trust you.

It's hard to admit, even to myself, that there are
    no easy answers to life's hard questions.

Help me to see things as you see them.

In wrestling with you, my imperfect faith is made
stronger.

In wrestling with you, I discover a deeper truth:
that my questions usher me right back to you.

Psalm 9:10

Those who know your name will trust in you,
for you, LORD, have never forsaken
those who seek you.

Dignity

I never wanted to be like this—dependent on
others for the most intimate parts of daily life.

Caregivers now do for me what I cannot do
for myself.

At times it is awkward and embarrassing.

I feel so exposed.

Where is the dignity in this?

Is there no choice but to grin and bear it?

Perhaps I have no choice, except in how I choose
to receive a caregiver's help.

When I am self-conscious, remind me that I am
made in your image, God.

When I feel shame, tell me once again that I am
precious to you.

Turn my humiliation to gratitude.

Talking with God in Old Age

Enfold me this day in a warm blanket of hope
and compassion.

And grant me dignity.

Psalm 25:1-3

To you, O Lord, I lift up my soul;
in you I trust, O my God.
Do not let me be put to shame,
nor let my enemies triumph over me.
No one whose hope is in you
will ever be put to shame,
but they will be put to shame
who are treacherous without excuse.

Falling

When you get old, you worry a lot about your
next fall.

Will it be the one in which you break a bone?

This frightening thought haunts me each day.

I've learned not to go anywhere without
my walker.

Even so, there are times when I'm caught
by surprise.

My head suddenly spins like a runaway top.

In the blink of an eye, my legs give way
beneath me.

My skeletal hand cannot stop the fall, and I
collapse to the ground, a crumpled mess.

I'm reminded of just how vulnerable I am.

Though I might I stub my toe and lose my
balance, though I might tumble to the floor
and fracture a bone,

I will never fall out of your reach, precious Lord.

Never.

Psalm 37:23-24 (NRSV)

Our steps are made firm by the LORD,
when he delights in our way;
though we stumble, we shall not fall headlong,
for the LORD holds us by the hand.

Surprise Me Today

I like surprises that make me smile inside—

out-of-the-blue moments that give a boost to
dry routine.

Like a sudden burst of warm sunshine on a
blustery afternoon,

an unexpected hug from a giggling toddler,

or an old friend standing at my door with a
loaf of warm bread and two plates.

Simple blessings that lift me up.

Things that remind me it's good to be alive.

You have scattered surprises throughout my
days, God.

I need only to open my eyes and ears.

Then I will notice the tangerine sun as it melts
into the horizon.

I will hear the sweet song of the caregiver who
hums while she makes the bed.

Help me to discover more surprises today,

And teach me to accept them with a
  grateful heart.

Psalm 66:5 (NLT)

Come and see what our God has done,
what awesome miracles he performs for people!

Alone

I still listen for the footsteps that do not come.

This is not how our retirement years were
    supposed to be.

We were supposed to grow old together—
    rock on the porch
    and visit national parks together.

But it didn't turn out that way.

After all this time, I should be used to the idea
    that I am solo.

Just one. No longer part of a couple.

It's not easy to be alone.

There are days when my heart sinks to my toes.

My mind clings to how life used to be.

On those days, even nice memories rest on me
    like a blanket of hot air.

        Talking with God in Old Age

And so I move through the routines of life
   behind a pasted-on smile,

feeling swallowed up by grief
   and all alone.

O God, take away this sadness as only you can.

Restore the joy that will get me through . . .

One day at a time.

Psalm 51:12

Restore to me the joy of your salvation
and grant me a willing spirit, to sustain me.

Kleenex in My Sleeve

I have a Kleenex in my sleeve.

I put a fresh one there each morning.

It's just a habit, I suppose.

A comfort, knowing it's there if I need it
    to wipe a tear, a nose, a spill.

And even though others may tease me, I keep a
    tissue where it is easy to reach,

    stuffed neatly into my sleeve.

In an odd way, it makes me think about you,
    Lord.

About how you are always within reach

    whenever I need you,

    even when I forget you are there.

Your presence is as close as the Kleenex
    in my sleeve.

Even closer.

Psalm 34:18

The LORD is close to the brokenhearted
and saves those who are crushed in spirit.

My Mind Seems Small

I can't hold back a giggle when someone has a
   senior moment:

   that dreaded time when you can't remember
   your neighbor's name,

   an embarrassing lapse in an already
   checkered memory.

But I admit, it's not so funny when it happens
   to me.

Before I grew old, I could recite every state
   capital.

I could rattle off the grandchildren's birthdays
   with ease.

Now thoughts bounce back and forth as I
   desperately search for facts I've known for
   many years.

And sometimes words simply refuse to come
   at all.

But even though I forget ordinary things, I
cannot forget all you have done in my long
life, God.

I give you thanks, knowing you are bigger than
my too-small mind.

Bless this cobwebbed brain of mine as I seek
you still.

Psalm 105:3-5

Glory in his holy name;
let the hearts of those who seek the Lord rejoice.
Look to the Lord and his strength;
seek his face always.
Remember the wonders he has done,
his miracles, and the judgments he pronounced.

Obituary

Every morning I drink my coffee and scan the
newspaper headlines.

Then I turn to the obituaries to see who has died.

On most mornings, the obituaries are about
people I've never met.

But occasionally there's a picture of someone I've
known for years.

It is a blunt reminder of my own mortality.

Date of birth. Date of death. In between, life.

In today's paper, there's an obituary for a bank
president who liked to skydive.

It makes me wonder what my family will say
about me when I die.

How will they sum up my long life
in a tiny space?

What will be important enough to say in a
column that costs a fee?

Talking with God in Old Age

Compared to celebrities and corporate
   executives, my life seems mundane.

And so I wonder if my obituary will
   go unnoticed.

Will it just be another one that strangers skim
   over while sipping coffee?

Somehow I think you care less about obituaries,
   Lord, than you do about how people live.

Help me to invest the rest of my life in things
   that will last long after I am gone.

In kindness and compassion. Integrity
   and gratefulness.

In loving you and loving others.

Show me how to live this day well, knowing that
   what I do today has eternal purpose.

Psalm 89:48 (NLT)

No one can live forever; all will die.
No one can escape the power of the grave.

Shut In, Shut Out

Maybe it sounds silly for someone as old as me to admit,

but my feelings are hurt.

I feel like a youngster who has been rejected by a more popular classmate.

No one comes to visit me,

at least not very often.

I know the excuses by heart—

how everyone is so busy these days.

But it hurts to think that I've been forgotten.

Even though I'm old and wrinkled, I still want to be included.

I want to hear about the family's goings and comings—

about how a grandson is doing in geometry

and what the baby is doing now.

Talking with God in Old Age

Sometimes it seems as though the windows on my old life have been boarded up, trapping me inside with no way to see the world outside.

On these days, loneliness is my companion.

So I lean on your promises, God.

That you are the giver of hope. The one who never forgets me.

Remind me that I am shut in, but not shut out.

Psalm 119:49-50

Remember your word to your servant,
for you have given me hope.
My comfort in my suffering is this:
Your promise preserves my life.

Tears

No one expects someone as old as me to cry,
but I do.

Usually I cry when no one can see.

I just lean against the shower wall and let the
tears fall, water against water.

Sometimes when I go to bed at night, I have a
private little cry.

The kind where tears slide sideways across my
face and onto the pillow.

Other times tears never come.

There's just a sadness that washes over me,
flooding my weary soul.

I wonder if anyone cares about what I'm going
through.

Does anyone really understand what it's like to
grow old?

Then I remember:

My tears are dear to you, God.

You understand when no one else does.

So tonight I will close my swollen eyes,

And tomorrow I will rediscover the joy of a
new day.

Psalm 30:5b

Weeping may remain for a night,
but rejoicing comes in the morning.

Good Good-bye

I watch the moving van pull up to the curb.

Another friend is leaving.

Moving to a new place, to be closer to family.

Once again good-byes have been said.

Strangely, I feel abandoned.

Left behind by those who have become my
    friends in these sunset years.

I wonder if I'll ever see them again.

It's so hard to say good-bye.

Even when you're old.

Especially when you're old.

Life has already been a long parade of farewells.

O God, help me guard against self-pity.

Show me opportunities to touch someone's life,

to stir up conversation.

to laugh together on this incredible adventure
of life.

I think there must be something good in
good-byes, for in the eternal scheme of things,

good-bye is only the beginning.

Psalm 49:15

God will redeem my life from the grave;
he will surely take me to himself.

Hearing Aid

Someone has hit the Mute button on my life.

I can see mouths moving, but there's no sound.

It's so frustrating to pretend you hear someone
when you don't.

Or to ask people to repeat what they've said.
Again.

Often I hear only snatches of conservations.

I guess at what words fit into the gaps of silence.

Other times, there's just annoying background
noise—

the kind that turns normal conversation
into babble.

So I try to adjust my hearing aid to filter out the
distractions,

hoping to hear with clarity.

Perhaps it's not that different with you, Lord.

How can I hear you when there is so much chaos in the world?

In this old life that brims with frustrations, prepare me to hear your voice.

Turn your ear to me.

Let my conversations with you spill over into daily life.

Then one day I will clearly hear the sound of heaven erupting in celebration.

Psalm 102:1-2

Hear my prayer, O LORD;
let my cry for help come to you.
Do not hide your face from me
when I am in distress.
Turn your ear to me;
when I call, answer me quickly.

Real Person on the Phone

I wish more real people talked on the phone
    these days.

I pick up the receiver and say hello.

An unfamiliar voice jabbers on about insurance
    or politics.

"Push one for this, two for that."

I listen just long enough to discover there's not a
    real person on the line.

Then I hang up.

This automated nonsense! I think.

Doesn't anyone care that I had to rush to my walker
    so I could get to the phone across the room?

I know to be skeptical of strangers,
    of frauds and slick schemes.

But whatever happened to the days when real people called just to chat,

to see how your day was going?

Real people with compassionate hearts.

Maybe I'll call an old friend today just to see how she's doing.

To remind her that this is the day you have made, God. Let us rejoice and be glad.

Psalm 118:24

This is the day the Lord has made;
let us rejoice and be glad in it.

Butterfly

I watched a butterfly flit by today.

It wafted on a gentle breeze and rested on a
flower just long enough to sip some nectar.

It closed its vibrant wings, then stretched them
out again before flying away.

Doing what you, the Creator, designed it to do.

I can't help but think about where the butterfly
goes in the storms of life—

when the wind blows and the rain pelts
the earth.

I think it must hide in the crevices between rocks
or under sturdy leaves.

A butterfly, so fragile yet somehow strong
enough to fly hundreds of miles.

Perhaps your colorful creature is a
gentle reminder

to do what you designed me to do—

to live in such a way that people will catch a glimpse of you.

Psalm 8:3-9 (NLT)

When I look at the night sky
and see the work of your fingers—
the moon and the stars you set in place—
what are mere mortals that you
should think about them,
human beings that you should care for them?
Yet you made them only a little lower than God
and crowned them with glory and honor.
You gave them charge of everything you made,
putting all things under their authority—
the flocks and the herds
and all the wild animals,
the birds in the sky, the fish in the sea,
and everything that swims the ocean currents.

O LORD, our Lord, your majestic name
fills the earth!

Standing on the Edge

Here I am, caught between a strong will to live
and a desire to quit trying.

I feel as though I'm standing at the edge of a
desert, a barren land where life has dried up.

It is a place I don't want to go.

For all these years I've resisted growing old, but
gradually, time has worn me down.

Now I feel as though I've shriveled up inside this
stooped body.

A drab sluggishness has crawled into my soul
and siphoned life away.

But as I spend time with you, God, I begin to
understand that long life is a gift,

not a punishment to be endured through
gritted teeth.

Still there are questions that beg to be asked.

How will I deal with the challenges of aging?

Talking with God in Old Age

Will I grow or will I diminish?

Here at the edge of the desert, I begin to make
peace with my timeworn body.

Psalm 63:1-3

O God, you are my God,
earnestly I seek you;
my soul thirsts for you,
my body longs for you,
in a dry and weary land
where there is no water.
I have seen you in the sanctuary
and beheld your power and your glory.
Because your love is better than life,
my lips will glorify you.

Waiting Rooms

Waiting rooms are strange places.

You are supposed to go there to relax while thumbing through last year's magazines.

Waiting for the person with a clipboard to open the door and announce the next patient.

I always dread hearing my name called, yet I am anxious to get it over with.

And so I wait.

I wait until they shuffle me off to another room, where I wait some more.

There I stare at the ceiling to pass the time.

There's a grid of square tiles, a few with water stains. Some with ragged edges.

There are vents and a smoke alarm.

Harsh fluorescent lights and medical contraptions.

I can hear the muffled voices of nurses and
doctors through the walls and closed door.

Still I wonder:

Why is waiting so exhausting?

*Doesn't anyone know how hard it is for an old person
to linger?*

When I am overwhelmed by waiting, Lord, refill
my reserves of patience.

And help me to remember that while I am
waiting, you are working.

Psalm 130:5-6 (NRSV)

I wait for the LORD, my soul waits,
and in his word I hope.
my soul waits for the Lord
more than those who watch for the morning,
more than those who watch for the morning.

Thick Ankles and Varicose Veins

I hear a lot of talk about growing old gracefully.

As if aging requires ballet lessons.

I can't even imagine squatting down with parentheses legs, heels together and arms arched overhead.

I can't bend like I used to.

In fact, it's hard to tell where my legs end and my feet begin.

My ankles are so thick now.

I must look like a cartoon character, hobbling stiff-legged and slow.

If I peel back the special socks I wear, there's a spiderweb of purple veins on my legs.

Yellowed toenails too.

It's a sight we old people know too well.

So I try to find the humor in advanced age.

I'll laugh about my thick ankles and varicose veins.

Then I'll slip my feet out of these stretched-out shoes and rest awhile.

Maybe another old one like me will prop up his set of thick ankles too.

Encourage us to keep going on this journey of long life, dear God.

Psalm 10:17

You hear, O LORD, the desire of the afflicted;
you encourage them, and you listen to their cry.

Brighter Side

They say growing old is not for sissies.

That is an understatement.

Those who think it's just about having a cheery outlook don't have creaking bones or chronic pain.

On some days, it's especially hard to see life with a glass-half-full attitude.

Blessings get folded in with the worries of the day until I lose sight of them.

Blessings that are the unique gifts of long life—

Gifts like holding the tiny fingers of a newborn great-grandchild

or discovering that the new resident is a childhood friend.

It's true that I'm a little down today, but I refuse to stay there.

I will wrap my arms of faith around the One
who will pull me up

to see the brighter side of life,

where laughter reigns over sadness;
where kindness overcomes depression.

Today I will be a cheergiver for someone else.

Together we will bask in the brighter side of life.

Psalm 42:5-6a

Why are you downcast, O my soul?
Why so disturbed within me?
Put your hope in God,
for I will yet praise him,
my Savior and my God.

What's for Dessert?

I like to play a little game with myself:

I try to guess what we will have for dessert
  each day.

I have favorites, of course.

Coconut pie and banana pudding.

I don't even mind the low-cal, sugar-free kind
  that makes you believe you're eating
  something sinfully delectable.

But whoever decided that applesauce qualifies as
  dessert is just flat wrong!

There is one thing I know for certain:
  most of us old ones look forward to dessert.

Why shouldn't we?

A dollop of whipped cream on fresh strawberries
  will perk up anyone's day.

Talking with God in Old Age

So I scope out dessert long before I've had a
single bite of salad, anticipating what's
to come.

I think about how dessert makes even a so-so
meal somehow better.

Now as my life draws to fulfillment, I smile when
I consider dessert.

Your word is sweet, O God.

I know the best is yet to come.

Psalm 119:103

How sweet are your words to my taste,
sweeter than honey to my mouth!

Funerals and Such

On most days I'm not afraid to die.

My papers are all in order—
   living will and medical orders too.

The funeral home contract is prepaid.

I've even selected the clothes I'll wear and have
   them hanging in a plastic bag at the end of
   my closet.

But whenever I mention death, my family plugs
   their ears.

They say it's too depressing, too morbid to discuss.

I say it's just a natural conclusion to life.

It seems the only people who talk easily about
   death are other old people.

And so we do.

We old people sidle up close to the topic and chat
   about our funeral plans.

We talk about caskets and how we hope to die in our sleep at home.

Over the years, I've learned that life is not about trying to be good.

There's something more to it than just being an upright citizen who gives to charity and pays the bills on time.

And so, I talk of funerals and such without fear or dread,

knowing you are good, O Lord, and I am yours.

Psalm 100:5

For the Lord is good
and his love endures forever;
his faithfulness continues
through all generations.

Still Kickin'

Lately I've been mulling over my long life.

Each morning, it's a surprise when I wake up to
my old self again.

Still breathing.

Still kickin', as they say,

though not as high as I used to.

My spine is not nearly as pliable as it once was.

Neither is my mind.

I privately wonder if I'm even teachable
anymore.

Have I learned all I can learn?

Is there something more I can do?

The questions strike a chord deep within me.

God, I don't believe you have put my life on hold
just because I'm old.

Help me figure out your calling for me at this late stage of life.

Reveal your purpose for me now.

And fire me up to get on with living.

Psalm 138:8

The LORD will fulfill his purpose for me;
your love, O LORD, endures forever—
do not abandon the works of your hands.

Broken Dreams

I don't like the land of broken dreams.

It's a place where hopes for tomorrow are piled
in a rusty heap.

There are dreams of places I never got to go,

of careers I never had.

of things I never did.

It is a dumping ground strewn with the rotting
remains of what might have been.

So why do I dwell in this miserable place?

Is it because I spend too much time looking at
life in hindsight,

lamenting each missed opportunity and every
what-if?

The world has a way of shattering fanciful hopes.

I never sailed the Mediterranean or stood on the
Eiffel Tower.

I never became the company president or got featured on a magazine cover.

O Lord, give me this day a gentle acceptance of unfulfilled dreams.

Help me see that my life has been full beyond measure.

You created something more beautiful than I could ever have imagined, using the jagged shards of my broken dreams.

You created a kaleidoscope of color that is uniquely my life.

Psalm 139:13-14

For you created my inmost being;
you knit me together in my mother's womb.
I praise you because I am fearfully
and wonderfully made;
your works are wonderful,
I know that full well.

Sometimes Life Stinks

Sometimes life stinks.

Like a three-day-old chicken left in a trash can on a hot day, it reeks.

In an instant, everything changes.

A spouse dies.

A grandchild gets cancer.

A stroke leaves you partially paralyzed.

Suddenly a nasty sensation congeals in your stomach.

Where are you, God, when life's journey takes me through last week's garbage?

When life seems so unfair?

I pour out my complaints and give an impassioned plea.

Remind me that you still care when my heart breaks.

Put gratitude on my lips until I feel
thankful again.

Reassure me that you are walking with me
through the stench of life.

Psalm 142:1-2

I cry aloud to the LORD;
I lift up my voice to the LORD for mercy.
I pour out my complaint before him;
before him I tell my trouble.

My Time, Your Time

Time is a funny thing.

It seems to drag on when life is hard,

but it rushes by in a blur when things are
 going well.

It's a mystery to me how the same sixty minutes
 can feel so dissimilar.

Now that I'm old, life seems to crawl on its belly
 like a slug.

Everything takes longer to do than before.

Even getting up from a chair takes several tries.

By the time I've completed one task, it's almost
 time to do it again, in reverse.

Like putting on my socks and shoes, then taking
 them off again.

I confess there are days when it seems this life
 will never end.

Talking with God in Old Age

That I'll be stuck in this worn-out body forever.

But then there are moments when I am amazed at how quickly time has passed.

My own children are now grandparents.

Time is a peculiar thing.

Even so, I am reminded that my time is not your time, O God.

You created it and know more about it than I do.

Though my mind will not stretch to a full understanding, I am confident that you are a God of perfect timing.

So give me energy to make the most of the time that remains.

And help me to quit staring at the clock.

Psalm 90:4

A thousand years in your sight
are like a day that has just gone by.

A Piece of Me

This afternoon I gave away a piece of me—
a favorite possession.

I gave it to a friend who has been kind to me for
a long time.

It was something I had always kept on a shelf.

Something worth more in sentiment than
money, I suppose.

Still, I had cherished it for many years.

But today I decided I wanted to give it away
while I still could,

so I dusted it off and wrapped it in
tissue paper.

I put it in a used gift bag and gave it to
my friend.

When I saw her eyes brim with tears, this old
body felt light again.

It's funny how good it feels to give yourself away.

Talking with God in Old Age

And though I gave away a piece of me,
   I somehow felt whole again.

Psalm 37:21

The wicked borrow and do not repay,
   but the righteous give generously.

Be Still

You'd think someone like me would be an expert on being still.

I spend so much time sitting in my recliner and resting on my bed.

Just being still.

Even so, I am very restless.

There's no blaring TV to disturb me.

No neighborly chatter to divert my attention.

Just a noise in my soul that keeps me on edge.

I'm led to wonder what impact my life has, now that I've grown old.

But it seems to be a one-sided conversation.

Is silence the language you speak, God?

Don't you have anything to say to this old one?

About long life and the challenges it brings?

About what will happen when I die?

And so I ask you to simply quiet my mind.

Help me to be still in your presence and know
that you are God.

Psalm 46:10a

"Be still, and know that I am God."

I Don't Like Change

I don't like change very much.

Meat loaf is on Tuesdays, and fried fish is on
Fridays.

The green plastic glass is for mixing the
powered medicine.

Last month's newsletter goes under the tray on
the table.

When you get old like me, change gets harder.

The world seems to turn so fast, I can't keep up.

There's little I can control now that life is fading
away.

I've left behind my home of fifty years.

Most of my belongings have been boxed up or
given away.

Lifelong friends have moved or passed away.

Now even the smallest change sends me into
a tizzy.

I feel like a defiant child, digging in my heels.

I fume and scheme, desperate to take charge.

Until at last I remember:

Though everything around me changes, you do
not, O God.

You are unchanging. Steadfast. Forever.

Psalm 102:27

You remain the same,
and your years will never end.

Surely

In my life, sometimes it has been hard to see
your goodness and mercy

in the midst of trials and tragedy.

I've often thought you didn't care, Lord.

But I was wrong.

Now I am standing on the far end of my life's
time line.

From this vantage point, I can look across the
span of time and see how you brought
goodness out of difficult circumstances.

Though I didn't know it at the time, you were
working to bring blessings out of pain.

And so I've learned that the more I know you,
the more I trust you.

Surely goodness and mercy will follow me all the
days of my life.

Not maybe or perhaps.

But surely,

certainly,

like an intoxicating fragrance that trails behind
this old life.

There's no mistaking who you are and what you
have done.

Now I can face the future with confidence,

knowing I have a place with you forever.

Psalm 23:6

Surely goodness and love will follow me
all the days of my life,
and I will dwell in the house
of the Lord forever.

About the Author

Missy Buchanan, a former creativity educator, lives in Rockwall, Texas, with her husband, Barry. She is the author of the best seller *Living with Purpose in a Worn-Out Body: Spiritual Encouragement for Older Adults.*

Missy writes a monthly column, "Aging Well," for *The United Methodist Reporter*. She has written articles for many publications, including *Presbyterians Today, Presbyterian Older Adult Ministry Network News*, and *Read the Spirit*.

Missy speaks regularly to older adult groups, churches, and women's groups. She has a special place in her heart for older adults after serving as a daily caregiver for her parents in their last years.

For more information, visit Missy's Web site at www.missybuchanan.com.